Laynie Browne writes the path forward in this luminous manuscript where language is alchemy, the mercury in a medium that dissolves and reconstructs the self by growing tendrils under her own banner. *Apprentice to a Breathing Hand* is a brilliant lyrical achievement.
— Brenda Coultas, author of *The Writing of an Hour*

"The women who ask bodies to be present and constant are dancers" —a proposition suggesting that significance and signification are ever-present, awaiting the activation of attention. Lyric address to a beloved "you," dilated to include the fictive, the plural, and the non-human is one such activation offered by *Apprentice to a Breathing Hand*. Also: the release of song and chant that harbor in speech alongside the histories that shelter in etymologies. Here we learn to believe in the agency of expansion and preservation, energetic forces by which the word and its selves blossom.
— Karla Kelsey, author of *On Certainty*

In *Apprentice to a Breathing Hand*, Laynie Browne has convoked an opulent meditation on feminist practice and presence. This is a book of the phenomenologies of intention as functions of the senses: the five physical senses, yes, but also the other senses, that drive the self towards the "calm words" that bracket both empathy and ephemerality. As far as instructions for living go, Browne "tries to explain" but prefers to show, after the manner of Julian of Norwich. The terms of "wanting yourself back" are dual: garner on the one hand, oracular on the other.
— G.C. Waldrep, author of *feast gently*

Apprentice to a *B*reathing *H*and

Text set in Balthazar, Garamond 3 LT Std, & Minion Pro

Cover, layout & design by Sharon Zetter
Cover art: *hands touching* by Laynie Browne

Printed in the United States
by Books International, Dulles, Virginia
Acid Free Archival Quality Recycled Paper

Library of Congress Cataloging-in-Publication Data

Names: Browne, Laynie, 1966- author.
Title: *Apprentice to a Breathing Hand* / Laynie Browne.
Description: Oakland, California : Omnidawn Publishing, 2025. | Summary:
"The poetry of Laynie Browne's Apprentice to a Breathing Hand explores
alchemy, connectivity, and perception. Throughout the collection, Browne
considers the formation and limits of personhood, the experience of a
body moving through time, and the imperative to continually learn and
unlearn. Browne looks to alchemy as a practice for cultivating the
impossible, positioning it as a fitting model for our current moment. In
the material of language, meaning must be unmade and remade endlessly,
and in this continual regeneration, Browne considers the alchemy of how
a poem can in turn transform the poet. Moving through methods of making
and unmaking, the collection centers on the figure of an apprentice
working in a space of indeterminacy, lack, breath, and constant
shifting"-- Provided by publisher.

Identifiers: LCCN 2024062333 | ISBN 9781632431615 (trade paperback)
Subjects: LCGFT: Poetry.
Classification: LCC PS3552.R748 A83 2025 | DDC 811/.54--dc23/eng/20250103
LC record available at https://lccn.loc.gov/2024062333

Published by Omnidawn Publishing, Oakland, California
www.omnidawn.com
10 9 8 7 6 5 4 3 2 1
ISBN: 978-1-63243-161-5

Apprentice to a Breathing Hand

Laynie Browne

OMNIDAWN PUBLISHING
OAKLAND, CALIFORNIA
2025

Also by LAYNIE BROWNE:

POETRY
Everyone and Her Resemblances. Pamenar Press. 2024.
Intaglio Daughters. Ornithopter Press. 2023.
Letters Inscribed in Snow. Tinderbox Editions. 2023.
Practice Has No Sequel. Pamenar Press. 2023.
Translation of the Lilies Back into Lists. Wave Books. 2022.
In Garments Worn by Lindens. Tender Buttons Press. 2019.
You Envelop Me. Omnidawn Publishing. 2017.
P R A C T I C E. Split Level Texts. 2015.
Amulets and Letters, Belladonna #173. 2015
Scorpyn Odes. Kore Press. 2015.
Deciduous Letters to Invisible Beloveds. Essay Press. 2014
Lost Parkour Ps(alms) 2014 Presses universitaires de Rouen et du Havre
Roseate, Points of Gold. Dusie Press. 2011.
The Desires of Letters. Counterpath Press. 2010.
The Scented Fox. Wave Books. 2007. (winner of the National Poetry Series)
Daily Sonnets. Counterpath Press. 2007.
The Desires of Letters. Belladonna #93. 2006.
Original Presence. Shivistan Books. 2006.
Drawing of a Swan Before Memory. University of Georgia Press. 2005.
     (winner of the Contemporary Poetry Series)
The Desires of Letters. Counterpath Press. 2005.
Mermaid's Purse. Spuyten Duyvil. 2005.
Webs of Argiope. Phylum Press. 2005.
Pollen Memory. Tender Buttons Press. 2003.
Gravity's Mirror. Primitive Publications. 2000.
The Agency of Wind. Avec Books. 1999.
Clepsydra. Instress. 2004.
L O R E. Instress. 1998.
Rebecca Letters. Kelsey St. Press. 1997.
One Constellation. Leave Books. 1994.
Hereditary Zones. Boog Literature. 1993.

COLLABORATIONS
The Complete Works of Apis Mellifera, with Bernadette Mayer. Further Other
     Books. 2017.
Nascent Toolbox, with Lee Ann Brown. Owl Press. 2004.

FICTION
Periodic Companions. Tinderbox Editions. 2018.
The Book of Moments. Presses Universitaires de rouen. 2018.
The Ivory Hour (A Future Memoir). Spuyten Duyvil. 2012.
Acts of Levitation. Spuyten Duyvil. 2002.

NON-FICTION
The Poet's Novel as a Form of Defiance: Indeterminate Frame. Kin Press. 2020.

for Mei-mei Berssenbrugge

Su despertar de mano respirando
de flor que se abre al viento

"Waking up like a breathing hand
like a flower opening to the wind"

Alejandra Pizarnik, *Diana's Tree*

CONTENTS

I.

Apprentice to a Breathing Hand

II.

Euphoric Rose

III.

A Self-Combed Woman

I.

Apprentice to a Breathing Hand

*E*lusive

i.

First advice, if you can't find your desk. Or you don't have a desk.
You still have to clear debris. First the horse's head, then the bird
outside the frame

Then the window. Then the one forsaken leaf, orange and
desiccated, caught in abandoned web

Push the calendar away from the floating heart given to you by
radiance of undoing

If your light falls adamantly forward, scarring your efforts, see this
as kissing paper

Look carefully at the fortunes pasted around you. If you find
carnelian, take off your hands

Place train ticket atop subway card atop golden folder atop
receipt, atop rags, atop regret atop a shell with a hole for
threading

Place your head inside notebooks you cannot bear to have born

Run away with yourself

If you've ever written breath you know exactly the color of ice
with live violets in centers, whispers

ii.

A message or an image may pierce the thousand small ailments

Sitting out of doors, note rising heat and maelstroms

A mind was on the ground, under the table, for everyone to see

We put on our best imitation of a person but it was not good
enough. We averted our eyes

We lay their writhing. *Poor thing*, we should have said, before
going on with our dinner. But instead, we said nothing

We excused our selves, climbed the stairs and locked the doors

And here we are sorting membranes from letters, hypotheses from
paintings

Leave us to our alchemy; forms will emerge

iii.

If you can't find your rest, or if you don't have any rest, you will
still need a place to be horizontal

Preferably beneath the lunar awning

I tried to explain this but my breath was silver and my hands I
could never find

You retrieve scraps of lace and place them to my lips as if to
reverse utterance

Leave me to sand, candles, bedding

My body, in my own possession, kept changing

What I sought was more elusive than shadow

*V*apor

Carry your egg, your vapor, up the stairs satirically

Embroider hammocks from ether. Fall to sleep suddenly but wake
slowly. Rotate each ankle before you step into moorings

Prepare your nest and allow yourself to steep

Three scoops of hibiscus, two of licorice. Don't measure the buds
of lavender

Ignore grains of sand or pollen in the back of your throat

Carry a flask carved from wood, a red liquid. Stain your dress with
ice

Small white flowers on a blue background in the bodice turn gold
and crimson

Take off your outer designs. Rub the fabric between your fingers
as you sink

Remove the memory of silhouettes from your posture

Pull a thin sheathe over your shoulders to remember the way
another described you to a mirror

Carry the night you gave your name to darkness across your
forearms

Then sit in front of that divining screen that separates you from your cursive body

Lift the glass and stain the frock of your consciousness

Each night walk through coarse air; breathe heavily, as if your neck wore burlap clouds

As if twinkling in the trees as you approach did not represent flight

Visit frogs sounding cows, trees spilling water, and the dirt path colored by the silent child

Open your throat until your mouth swells with darkness

Coax

Conjure milky lunar winds. Leave your outline behind. Images
faint, pose as dolls, paperwarm

Overrun sacrosanct maps. An absent place steals powers. Singes
violet. Insists in stark vellum. Printing sans color reduces
drawings to scales of gray

I never planned to be a feather, a peony with fallen head, gown
drawn on, translucent. My texture was quiet and unprintable,
delicate pencil tracings

Ink is less costly than cloth. Petals more volatile than names. Talk
through proofs, before galleys. Images we see simultaneously are
most useful

A door is pinned open. Ghost translates marginalia into cafés.
Drinks from verses and annotations

Roan light falls onto circular tables, illuminates a desk, stands
in a doorway. Three shadows sit on a fence. Do you hear their
rippling?

Stay lost—waiting for words to come alive as they enter your
mouth. Like carbon, looking into a mirror

Red liquid, pink glass, engraved with incantations. Coax dusk,
letters, thread. Stand under awnings hewn to invite

An alphabet is a sturdy audience. A candelabra of lunar hands

Thread

Vice is in—advice. Inside thread is—read, and red. Also, dear—

A mind made of drills, a tentacle audience, personal scarlet,
potions of temporality

Do you squint as she approaches, toward large glass walls,
carrying needle and broom, carrying music tied soundly to lack?

Will you revolve acres on paper, paste onto envelopes? Invite
beams of light to kneel?

Have you ever written instructions to yourself, bereft of
apprentices?

Do you remember how to singe fine power, how to turn twinge to
dawn?

How to rise up and twist threads together until they learn to
cling—until—like letters you find your strand

*E*rasure

A sage of the rose family draws red vibrations with breath

A crowned snake deserves your full attention

Seeks emptiness, runs toward an uninhabited room, in tears of elation

An empty egg remembers sweeping forms braided from light

Remembers the return of maidens, palpitations, nocturnal sapience

Erase yourself to know a former— _____ cannot be found in reflection

Engage remedies to aid this process, not to stop—

Movement toward sepia labyrinth with vials: bloodroot, phosphorus, wind-flower

See yourself through every guise, as stones approach

I laughed at overdoing while unpacking an imaginary terrace—of gossamer

If I lived in a world safe for women—

When you wake with non-visible parts broken. In a non-matrifocal culture, as an infant crone. Torn wing and tongue.

Affection is also filmy gaze, smashed curtains trailing

Hurling reveries as we stow ethereal limbs above

Molten

She marks on her silken calendar when to molt. A woman before
going to bed, yet every night, a river

Warm skin in skein, wanders, causal arrival

How to wilt, in profusion—hydrangea. Glide to soil—as molten
slip

Eyelets cover her entire ideation

Recline into silence, into the unconscious, but we don't use that
word; we use the name of an animal

Night covers her like sand and silt, like water

Every night is a session of spikes, repetition, closing of obsidian,
still lashes

An underground bird, talked into a drawer, a sleeping elevator,
stuffed inside a sock, a trance, a garment, a tent

Who placed her inside this vessel?

Was it a hand small and luminous, impossible to name?

And if she was entirely lost in the day at least when she lay down
in this river of cotton, this river of creased and perplexed flash

At least when she closed Saturn, at least she did not need to travel

the question—who she was: a series of fits, permutations pierced
by a seamstress, one could only call nascent selves

A substance otherwise opaque as night

Smudge

A vase with a vantage, a face. Why move and stand, flame. When
you cannot gain traction, as if the moment does not exist

Too small for anonymity we rotate, order, attempt to keep this
picture. Ducked under hair to notice a person who could see with
back of head. A pale distraction.

A knee, a word, a station unrelenting. Curve around the inner
curve—was a euphemism. Unable to understand magnetism or
deletion.

I won't say how or why I might use those streets, or cars behind
me. Persons we've never met washing, cradling, lisping. Is the door
locked? Can I leave at any time?

If I go now will I know where I was, who I am? Almost unbearable
battery of roses

You borrowed my names, my mane. Buried under the weight of
books—escorted my hand

The end is when we don't have a pen, and corners of eyes mere
smudges

Forsaking bloom. Dear stave, when overtaken, murmur your
subject opening

Come back when everything closes, where we embed our inventors,
coil and place balls of yarn by their sides in caverns of ravished song

Vivid

Enter this cocoon, a cave of breath free from tending to others

Empty of seething sun, rest your blood, until you are only waves.
Inside a shell, an open palm

As though blowing out a candle you become vivid, a name for red,
a ceremony

In her bundle she carries the first secret, sun roses, solitude

Inside a pink cloud describe yourself as fetal. A feathered aura
permitted to linger. Invite seven directions, beneath the lunar
awning

Yellow butterfly pressed against sight, against backdrop of
verdancy

Ask for their blessings as you turn

*B*ranch

Be sure of your arborescence, the root of any vertex, one direct path from u to v

Who you are in relation to crystalized silver, a quarter of an hour, clear water

Pray this amalgam, so called by alchemists, in relation to being tested

Stirred, poured into solution, dissolved, kept in a glass vessel, well-stoppered

Wading place—theorized, with fruit on branches

Where we know the dangers of confinement, lost and alive

Cognizant of the repetition of endings, and the one death which guides us

How to go astray, aslant, astral, where we still have limits yet leave the whole at rest

Where you are inside 'I', an ounce in a small vial, a notion with no firm attachment to any singular person. Add gold or silver, soft as butter

Appearances take forever: combed flowers, groomed names. Filaments thrust out into branches. Arise from mercury—tree

How to be multiple, dendritic, how to hear soothsayers, how to say anything transparent, wilting, essential to want—as one and separate

Still part of the same spirit-coat we suspend from outstretched branches—embodied, belonging and free

Coral

Kept alive by color, because we don't live alone

Provide shelter and you will be given light equivalent to food

Tissues convert ultra-violet to green shields, just below the water's surface

In deeper water, the blue part of the spectrum radiates red and orange

Glows to receive more sun

When language is dying how do we speak to our ancestors?

Grow armor diligently, secreting skeletons finer than thread

During the part of the day corresponding to ebb tide face magnetic south

Elongated aragonite crystals under a helium ion microscope pair a biological compass with internal tide clock

Long needle-shaped crystals, far from the mother plant, distinguished by length of arms

Our lungs we fold deftly—migrating feeding to marrow

Crossing

I saw the dangers of being in body, and translate

Hundreds of miles below the surface—castles

On the way home, heads green

Goats perched high in argan trees

Fish dressed red against water

Two dark eyes, mounted on a head-like mantle

Low hills with no ink sacs, no interior

Kissed the flesh of corals

Treeless woods use every list

Trace sworn, one who stands by, defender

Twin pillars, props of a mast, pots, shells

From the root of cup, weave vessel from willow

Who else dreams of words as crossings to fix or fasten

Vex, afflict, to lay one thing across another is still fiction

My edge, you crossed my corner, my border

Sword, over and over, crux

A path with reference to winds and ships

Until I became water, much too hard to track

Versification of stone, more siren than story

Face of eyelash, sepal, crystal-liniment

Séance until all content in discontent—departs

Dance

Two dances were occurring at the same time. I wished to attend
both but this was the dance of one self, dividing from another

A child is born of the body of a mother and goes on

Women dance in long strands flecked with blue glitter

One carries percussion, hitting a wooden cylinder. A dance with
thin clouds

I sat on the floor, in the bare dawn, with no other audience, no
invitation or direction

When the rehearsal ended the choreographer came up to me and
said the name of my child; I was a mother of music.

The leader approached two women and complained they had
missed practice. It's too early the other said. It's too early, the next
repeated, as a question, looking into her face. It's too early, she
said again. I imagined she had a small child she could not leave

I want to say they held harps but they did not hold harps. I saw
no costumes beyond long hair faded, like dripping moss

Their faces were solid and showed no expression. Their feet were
very light, deliberately dragging across the wooden floor making
patterns as they strode, turned, looped, moved across the large
space and then I was holding a book of ice. The dance was
otherworldly, trailing, and completely compelling

Moss hair, like that which hangs from cedars, hands dripping and lilting as they spoke with their bodies

Is this the dance one sees as a child departs childhood? Is there a dance for a person who is a paragraph to one's children leaving? Did they draw themselves before they left?

A dance for mothers with clouds, saying nothing, moving as dust and light

Twirling as the dance recoils inside bodies, made visible

As if the dance were a drawing of our features newly made, as we attempt to discern edges

As if we had no choice in the dance but to be all of these women

The ones who spoke with their feet making contact with the ground

The ones who did not speak at all, pliable, sinking, listening

The women who ask bodies to be present and constant are dancers

They breathe and move in relation to each other and this space of night and wakefulness

The women require costumes because their bodies are covered with names

We must be all of these women intimating, not carrying harps

Collapsing sounds we do not hear, as bodies arc in waves, like plants in fields

We are all of these women whether we reside in a warehouse or in the night air with crickets

Glitter in hair imagining the music of Meredith Monk

Voice as instrument sometimes recalls, permits or withholds—as a form of protection

Who is she protecting?

Were they dancing the drawings made by young adults with their parents on large sheets of rain before setting out to locate their future selves?

A dance of multiple selves, bereft of mothers, rafts across a wooden floor

Volition

Having forgotten who I was it did not help to look at a picture of
hands

No time without borders, brokenness, absence of light, reframed
sky

Having forgotten which direction I walked down an avenue of
foxes, given everything

Having read sentences as if they were unreal

Trust your other body, the one lingering, not yet born

Apprentice to a hand (like the woman whose hand acted without
her volition)

She sat down with the intent to read herself into sensation, away
from thought. Long since she had been inside language

A spell longer than a breath (*no, I'll never understand*) kept
intruding

She wished to construct existence within language, far from other
concerns, like emotion held in place beneath skin

How to abruptly leave certain sections of thoughts behind as if
they were belongings

How to recline in trench of light and take in words with the body until every unnecessary sentence has been replaced with another.

Until the body is weightless, removed from pictures the mind escapes

She lay there, inside her person, a person she hardly knew, and wondered how she might leave evenings void, emptying into nothing

Loneliness is a strong wish for solitude

Mantra

The curtain beside me in the library is a girl in stiff muslin dress.
Pale light drifts through beige-white swathes, the grain of a desk

Because my thoughts were poisonous I carried a paper list, a
spare translucent skin. The labyrinth of a large sunhat, concentric
circles above my head

As ink touches page I subtract myself from absence. Take each
thought behind speech or action and place it where I can easily see
and transmit

Outside a body of sinuous lines, rearrange your mantra, until
poison in appropriate dosage becomes food or medicine

A mantra is a voice with no body. Seek this sound where you are
mottled, feed on dislodged utterance, whatever falls into your
mouth. Where you are partially buried in sand or gravel, retracted

I kept my poison—taught myself to speak its tongue

What touches my lips is not only willing and imaginary, but also
billowing, an abundance of mist creatures continually reforming
along the surface, acrobatics we call subliminal

I'm placing your name inside my mouth where it rests in silence,
where darkness corresponds to warmth

I cried on the short walk over from cottage to library. Relief of
drinking pure air, invisible, infused with water, light, calm notes

Taste madronna and hemlock mixed with volcanic, intuition of molten centers, rising up along the spine, flight and the soft feet of foxes

Between myself and these steps toward water since last summer posed the dark winter, sharply unexpected loss, stipulations of a body to find order, resonances that would allow independence. There was also the sale of several childhoods, handfasting and blankness requiring doors of accommodation

On the ferry winter was famished and then gone, not even a form of wind, and as I stepped out toward the railing you took my picture—unrecognizable as a creature away from the mainland

You said the words, "otherworldly" and "tendril." "You" was not a mantra, but followed in wake, gathering crinolines, the other goodbye, knowing we don't depart from a single year's growth, cross section of ring, sapling water of those who reside in subliminal-forever

There is only now, and later, and soon. Time was not the brother I never had, never the friend or the lover. Rime was never parent— but a story, in waves transported us to sleep

II.

Euphoric Rose

Euphoric

I have this fantasy of we
travels with you under another sign
another name to say
that which is possible in multiple
where you already live
A place where bodies are defined
as something other than time
In this dream we endlessly molt
We wear a skeleton undressed yet
never separated from skin
We live within a ring described by moons
and love an atmosphere from which we do not divide
Etheric soil of home
Euphoric voice of hands

Euphoric Rose Acrostic

Even beside non-ethereal
Under rose lunation
Personhood deserted
Her until she spoke no common language
Of remedial words blades, emblems
Reuerye weaxen, weg, wassen
Illusory torch, pitch
Closest to ring

Ripped from skin, beam, shine
Once loved claw
Stranded crescent eye
Every lucent vow

Euphoric Rose

According to the same laws by which stars shine I have this fantasy of we, space to spread out, unbothered by bodies of bright ships, waters or waking.

Walking a path defines eyes stuck beneath map, beneath children, between paginated husbands.

I open the door to the sea, one kiss on each cheek. You don't know me.

A wisp floating was never your idea of a girl returning books to metal shelves. The baby deer cries loudly until I turn my head. A child screams and a mother tries, but fails, to ignore her.

Cries for who you were, who one might be. Eventually she picks up the child.

I've put on my hat and glasses in the seaside library. Everything is too bright, except my decision to begin earlier, to rush into language.

They said good morning fondly as if feeling were not invisible. A circle punctuated by wonderful births and implausible endings.

My soul radially whorls out to the edges of my body, travels with you under another sign

I seal my intention to think less poisonous thoughts by following a path of letters

Book as medicine. Words as nectar guides, illuminating the lips of flowers, visible to any reader.

Italics make us thankful that our existence is not solitary

Learning to thrive as inner pendulum swings from oneness with others to separateness is not as easy as pleading with feet, threading the crescent above eyes, or placing your body by the edge of living waters.

Water doesn't lack confidence; is bursting with forms feeding and reproducing. We give thought to these practices because we require care.

Our children require the inner heavens of probability, bodies we only possess by virtue of the forgetful acts of mountains.

We did not know we contained mountains.

You take a photograph of a vantage and possibly never again view the picture. Yet the image of the water is still contained in a non-visual replica you retrieve through breath.

A sumptuous interior extends beyond outlines. Where you write the color 'blue' and suddenly see what is bluer than blue, more sky than sky.

A color I see clairvoyantly, another name to say, my finger is banded in miniscule points of light

Every night your body fills with stars and reclines. I find myself along the edge of your breakage, between one inhalation and the next.

I'm here, fully awake, alive for love

In stages I move closer and closer to the land. First in my cottage, then walking toward the library.

Looking out on the sound, then, just outside the library on the deck, then out onto the knoll an old wooden chair

Until there is very little distance between my body and the water. Only air and light. A few feet further and I would be submerged

One oak edges the water, madronna and evergreen

Eventually I sit exactly on the earth, in an impression in the rock lined by gold grass, where I sat yesterday and the day before

Beneath the banded sky, though stars are not visible in daylight we know they are present

They speak to the water, one tiny moon, and movement along the surface of light

Light frequencies of the flower, that which is possible in multiple

In the morning they appear as rapidly moving white ripples. At night, when reflected by moonlight they appear silver. Have I ever seen this exact shade of blue?

I move to the ground so as to be closer to the color

Gold moss, empty stalks of hawkflower, past blossoming, and sheep sorrel. Pale green lichen on charcoal stone

Rocks in the water are sometimes birds; bull kelp appears to be the head of a seal. Today, blue on the water is tomorrow

Blue multiples scattering across what I imagine to be the brain, electrical impulse, firing

This impression in the earth was made for pause, one location of stillness

The blue electrifies mind, escorts us toward an edge, the place I'd like to exist, not glimmering surface but under the lid of the eye—water-retina, iris

A boat moves past and toward the future. A figure stands on deck, an arboreal line, with leaf-mast raised

Blue continues to explode along the surface, like the afterimage of pleasure

The closer we are to the land the more we enter—spin—with liquid color

Blue lights almost touching—now—leaping up onto the knoll to populate shores

The entire rose, where you already live. I want nothing between myself and the land, between myself and water, between myself and your breathing hand

Come—sit beside me, your aura and roots wrap round

Roots beyond the one who originated the myth you inhabit. It isn't the way you look in a photograph, but the way your face brightens in constant motion

I stretch my bare feet out in front of me on the moss and think of you

In that insatiable moment we almost twist toward and around each other, faces affixed

Try to place invasive thoughts in locations where they fail to breed

What I want requires depth, the opposite of ephemerality

Constancy requires a truthfulness befitting the unreal, so I'm better off as a plant turned toward water, thinking of you

A place where bodies are defined, *a small bud emerges, as if cupped by hands*

To write to and for and with and from is euphoric rose

To write in company is "we"

Bodily company of poem

Illusion that anyone has written in a solitary state is forgetting plant intelligence

Your listening eyes opened

Words scrawled in indistinct places I did not know I contained

Euphoric rose lives in your hand as it opens and breathes

Rose in palm, in eye, dreams

I look up away from the page, and see you for the first time

Listening with gaze until past-future unfurls

As something other than time, *petals, innumerable, sumptuous*
euphoros, bearing well, from bher, to carry

Let me begin with euphoria. The initial meaning, responding well
to medicine, from *pherein*

To write in frond and foam, in foremothers, where petals unfold,
open your hand

Foremost I am here to give you my neck, my sling, catapult,
casting net

To offer brier, bramble, half-cloyed eye, rose of flesh

A poem in rows borrowed from rozenwater, knot of ribbons, scent
of freshly cut wood

In this dream we endlessly molt, *future sense opening*

distance between the girl who enters a dark wood

in the middle *libationem*, in search of an oracle

and the woman who locates flight

Is this the same distance as from garden to string

Garland from noun and counting

Inundation bouquet, *urresian*, to rise

Each evening at dusk we enter hope of revolt

Pull lament toward filament house—pluck summons

Seed sub-rosa, aspenglow before dawn, after dusk

Search for beak of barred owl, peluchier, piluccare

We wear a skeleton undressed—*light can become coherent*

More likely you called her eglantine, sweet briar, dogrose

Diminutive needles about her throat

She pierces any domineering portrait

Torn through dark resinous skies, she plies

Blood or choice spirit, red approaching emptiness

Once, twice, thrice, she entered the wood at night

She knew the owl, though they never met

Sought to molt, subtract transparent distance

Between herself and euphoric rose

Never separated from skin *impressions like fingerprints*

In heraldic descriptions she wears a neckpiece of red fur

Several throats, or possibly you mistake poetical fancy

For—her mouth is not that diminutive flower

We live within a ring described by moons, *whereas for the rose,*
scarlet itself is matter

Salish Sea, rose gold, as in night, gold-blue mornings

After exodus of mist creatures, mountains unfurl, oreads

She visits an octopus before beginning, sees hiddenness, rubs her
body over land

Threads a night needle with nouns, her person/hood,
entanglement

Underwater the moon is troubled with orange smoke

Unsung—she wonders how to enter thicket, disc of night

Draw back fir curtains

Whereas for the moon, silver itself is tongued

The rose communicates instantly with the woman by sight, loves an
atmosphere from which we do not divide

Abbreviates to enter—*ule*, owl

Wuwalon,   *wwila,*   *ulula*

The bird proverbially and figuratively employed

in the appearance of ironic gravity

does not note persons up late at night

She was the imitation of a wail

Ululation, a hollow, a howl

Thus she became *nown, lollow, wollwe*

Etheric soil of home, *affinity between awareness and blossom*

She entered dull bluish-green, then bright, gleaming unspelt. She was not a grey-eyed goddess, nor was she a kite. She could not hover in the air like a bird, or dismissive invitation.

She entered the wood to reason, count, to tread thought, to attend. She entered to advise, counsel, persuade—an absence

She read to the owl sparagmous mummery, pertaining to ceremony, lustral soma

Euphoric voice of hands, *like seeing Venus in the day*

The root of her words espoused the wood, *abluere*, invisible wing

Aouren, apprentice of palm and hand

Blestian, bloedsian, blosison

Marks with *blotham*, blood,

Wen, wyscan, rhymes with night[1]

1"Euphoric Rose" is inspired by Mei-mei Berssenbrugge's book *Hello, the Roses*. Italic text (in the first line on every page) is from the title poem.

Euphoric Rose, A

Escalade scaragdos gem, green bareqeth
Umlaut, hludaz, to hear, upsilon
Polus, end of axis, heavens
Horizontem, bounding circle, marking stones
O eyn, khoreia, zero, shape of mouth
Reudh, trilled like growling burr
I voiced a pharyngeal fricative
Crescent, written ceilings, beds of chalk

Rare phoneme pence
Openian—gates, eyelids, epen
Secretus sesamum
Entrance of wound, cinder, bheue

Aeolian, ends of words changed

III.

Self-Combed Woman

Anchor

In a letter to our interior, the one unspoken, I asked an anchor to find me, typed endlessly in sanguine water up to my waist.

Asked place to come apart inside bodies repeatedly, like lifting a boat, like children no longer children row through ulterior tides with unduplicatable thoughts.

Eventually we relinquish autonomy and seek a sturdier body kept out of reach, one we diagram in blue air, anoint secretly.

The land is ancient yet the same as the inside of your hand.

I woke with this image of a word. Does word itself carry image?

Can we see inside perforations pierced through dark skies, through vapor and vacancy?

A passport into words, as more than signs, is also a language, a series of greetings in which we press our hidden bodies into a creature of many arms and names.

When I woke I saw supernal words, magnificent names, the center of the word sun.

I tasted your mouth not once, not twice, not within impermanence.

I tasted the center of every word and inside the sound was your name.

In my mouth inside the centers of rowing flowers, embers.

The water is almost golden, not separated from sky, the color of
borrowed hands.

Water mirrors the movement of impossible clouds, one thick
sheet invisible, swaths of sky, membranes

Above are the sleeping coniferous beings, below the vaster speech
of crowned words

Coral below lip

Water is turning inside itself to lift seed sounds, reversible pelagic
bodies lifting and falling

When I woke inside reverence of veins and trailing limbs

Halo face and burnished flame

Barred

Noiselessly through the canopy, mottled white and brown

Underparts marked with vertical bars on pale background, upper breast crossed with horizontal lines

I placed the book beside me, in front of my eyes, like a headlamp, to votive my way, hoping to séance your name, and simultaneously, to never surface

Hoping to wing and tail, hoping to roost quietly by day, to live in mature forest of deciduous and evergreen, often near water

To nest in tree cavity overwhelmed by the lexicon; to feed on words

Waters are still gold inside a story I make up and send as if it were morning inside glades of felt, absolutely alone—truth unbarred

'Courtship,' as a title, is too brief, too informal in terms of the ways I want to pearl one text to another, yet we become lost in endless import, nimbus of radiance

Don't let imagined dialogue overwhelm you. It's impossible not to be lost inside the nest which is already lostness, coil of feather and rag

I refuse to pluck and prune a finished replica. I give you what you might extract and set out in sun, much more than you expect, one tiny shard of shell

A red thread, translucent scripts of madronna unfurling, a place you've never been

Barred owls call to each other, vociferously, through cedar and hemlock. Brace your neck and look up

Will I ever find you? And the spell I place on a limb that you be potently inset, nuance and resin

Grasping bark with bill and talon, flapping, walking your way up trunk to take up residence in unfragmented rising

Owls are easiest found in forests at night, asking who will provide alchemy of fire, saucepan, and water. What am I doing here, can anyone tell me?

*R*emedy

Sewn beneath eyelids, closes looking

yet prism-eye tastes music: city sought; sea cast

Warmth, when splashed with insufficiency

is an incapacity to name

Words to hear and then to go home with, fiery

Until you learn to disappear whorls

only for short instants interior to whole

We being one; we being—momentarily

Disappear—extend long enough that we might—

Later is an excuse, a ruse, foremost, flailing

Moments well-behaved by water are gone

Pulsation, stops—not euphoria of letters

Do you know any calm words?

Do you see how this leads toward a precipice?

Yet, how to turn with no aisle on either side?

Like a featherless child a long way from bone

Facility with which you speak, flower to follower

Like a rudderless wind go where

Bright, like any animal, into the irresistible

Atomizer of time a long way from known

If you want yourself back—garner—oracular.

A Self-Combed Woman

i.

Unpromised, with long braid down back
Kombid, cembam, unkept, combed
When married, her mother rolls plait up to affix
Self-combed women chose to coil their own
Hair signals oath: camb, crest, honey, kambaz
Abandoned red garments of bride
Steps over threshold, to needle and weft

ii.

As silk rose, they found ways to be rid of feudalistic

Kam, kamm, kambr, toothed, scribal carpets

The self-combed women lived together

Even fathers or brothers required permission to enter

Cotton pulled from worsted cloth, forbidden italic

If she changed her mind she would be drowned

Lathe, notched scale, curling wave, ransom

She cannot die in a relative's home, nor be buried near

A homeless ghost, she may marry a dead man

Ghombhos, from gembh, bitten silvery presence

iii.

When silk fails she moves to Hong Kong or Macau

To Southeastern Seas, becomes a maidservant

Words recited with strokes of a comb—

First stroke, for luck, second for longevity

Outside the hall of ice and jade, men sought her

She implored them to depart, to make no demands

She fled poverty, forced betrothal, gamblers, opium addicts

Worked long hours, slept beside her machine

Connected and reduced curve, irreducible wood

She paid others to read aloud her letters

Recited from memory—aerial weaving comb, beautiful hand

iv.

Clandestine reading at night, in disguise

Abandoned false-bride plots

Search—rake over with comb

She adopts daughters in old age

Heraldic edging, voiced in gold letters

Female consciousness, her veiled body

Intrinsic muslin, handkerchiefs, blankets, bedding

Teeth intersect handle at a single point

Unequal to unique intersection of any other[1]

---

1 The term "self-combed woman" refers to a cultural phenomenon of
marriage resistance in the Pearl River Delta in Southern China between
the late nineteenth and early twentieth century. "Self-combed" women
chose independence and life-long chastity. Marriage law in 1950 by
the Communist state granted women more equality, thus ending the
practice.

Cloak with *Eyes*

i.

Time shivers and borrows—staggers—cloaks resuscitation

Heading into the woods she rarely looks over her shoulder.

The danger of looking back, into her tale, is the cloak of hair
behind her, covered in eyes, self-complement of strands.

The past competes with her sense of oneness.

List of absent beloveds is the tangle of needles—ahead and behind

Snares dried by heat of coal fuel, pine stoves, paraffin torch

Spirit sickness, mask of drowned women hung in beamed sky

Faint abandoned forms, imbroglio

ii.

She saw her station in reverse, affection for the self-combed woman

She wanders not the ground or other glasses, boats crisscrossing
her face, soundlessness

She wonders why she could never keep notions cut away: sister,
wife, daughter, mother forms fallen to bracken, eclipses donned
and discarded, exhausted

She rearranges soiled selves, foists devastated remainders, spends
herself in darkness constructing unopened disclosures

When constricted her body instructs her to walk out of doors,
away from the requirements of lace and tissue marrow, resin and
tar, foamy liquid throng.

iii.

She takes herself farther from the distance she dissolves, beyond
slipping-fathers, names he no longer remembers, beyond
evaporated-mothers, cloth-daughters, diaphanous familiars

Velvet worms and fungi illuminate travail

She wonders how else to estrange, cordon heart

Even with interminable distance thrust between each thought
grief returned readily, ran along the crests of non-waves

Radius flame unfathomable, found her

Every line a trigger, gold water

*U*lulation

They loved the owl more than ridiculousness. They went for a
walk looking for owls and emerged owl-headed, un-rustling.

They called to owls but saw only hovering foxes

They were so disappointed it didn't matter that no one had ever
before seen sky-foxes

They tried to be light, failed

Everything was distant except for the land

They begged expansiveness, breath-spirits

Seals and passages, beyond return, at the threshold

They walked beyond non-place to unsound

Nesting

I woke helpless, covered in white down, with eyes closed. I'm told the egg was pale, with rough surface of swamps, stream-sides, uplands. The moon was orange with smoke, dust and pollen.

To present day viewers residential nests are like picture postcards. They remind us of a unique living style of a bygone age.

Typical features to be found in a nest include a half-height screen door, a sliding floor with horizontal stars, carved woolen screens, etched feather windows and twig spirals.

With the passage of time signs of wear have appeared on matting, mud and ornamental leaves.

Once functional, trees have now become witnesses of beheading and uprooting called 'development.'

My nest was in a natural cavity, in an old forest with dead trees, in the distance between self and face. A whirled head, fledgling.

Recent decades have seen the demolition of many nests and rarely the refurbishment of their interiors.

Architectural components of old-styled nests from those demolished residences face total oblivion. I have succeeded in preserving some and include them in this exhibition.

First I prepared the story surface, then learned to strike intruders with feet. I preserved some nests by burying them in pockets, others by lacing third eyes.

I learned to wear nests on my head, to translate duets, cackles and haws.

I learned to store narration in the crook of a branch, or the top of a snag, to swallow whole, head first, and then body.

Mist

Mist opens across sound. Where it touches the surface it arches up, like a mother departed in shrouds.

She wraps herself in curtains, musings, in the ethereal.

Mutterings, here allow anything to happen

She wanted to enter the passage, both the wake of letters and the train of the ferry

She stops and starts and soon will be entirely absent of morning shoulders

The way complaint stands in the way, with no sense of your personal space, until we learn to flip the negative.

Stand up and walk toward awake mist beings.

Now I'm reading, now I'm seeding. Don't be dead—please.

Admiration, a spell.

Mist spreads out and rises in waves. Can everyone hear them walking?

When motion appears erratic, do I close the door to the sea?

Bodies do not last long enough to tell you, touch you, and yet you are present far longer than mist.

I wanted just to sit with your face in my hands. Pause and look.

Rushing is tantamount to who we are, any time

I keep wanting to be alone to do anything and then the aloneness is broken until it is not even worth having. Like mist bodies disappearing mid-morning

Like persons who talk too much, or don't talk at all; they don't appear actual. And then they disintegrate, whether or not you took the time to know them

Stillness and concentration, require stillness and concentration

Come, wake me. Make me up

It's cold and I'm closing the door, even though the sea is so seductive

My overlook is reading

There will be time (for remember) with a v

Rememver adds verdancy to a field of water, where so much life is invisible

I eat cherries and read your book, trying hard not to stain the pages

Painting is a Name for Moving Surfaces

i.

Un-spelt *wurdan* unfastened l e t t e r s—oars

Rudders we learn like sunlight falling onto faces

Painting as an imaginary relation with real persons

Colliding at night to caress features

Heaven below eider sky emerges

From land, lingers over spines

Lips move lightly on water, brows

Fog, curtains wave, commas surface

Walking-boats, spindles and legs

ii

When I cannot find lavender-dusk emptiness—of libraries

Faces and names, subtle organs, that which you make

Invisible—painting is the unseen—becoming sight

Images are triggers—realms we dare not name—theory baffles
thorns

Claws hair, wakes along wandering books—*sleb, slepaz*, sepal-sleep

Window-gold mistaking water for folded notes—to invisible
plum trees

Some artists write the illegible to make misunderstanding

Real—to name the places we lack. I don't

Believe in lanced color, separate from ether, spindrift

I read to waters, nightly

Reclined speaking in lines from books

As if darkness were those spines opening, turning, closing

iii.

Take a picture of the middle of the page

Begin with fortunetelling, fold

Slips, shapes, bokiz, beech—that books were once trees

Birch and ash, librum, inner bark of grove

We—as ruined garments (wrote from painting)

(*look-look* into rivers, garments, eyes, and sew)

We'd drunk only air

iv.

To paint in collage, kaleidoscopic gear, in foaming fonts

I only know how to spell sounds, not words
How to converse with spun air

Painting is a mane for moving surfaces
Painting is a name for unlaced water
Lit beneath
Painting is a name

v.

Spell yourself of scents
Letters, dirt memorabilia
Crushed over the body
Bath of irregular speech
Painting is anointing inner
Lids—as eyes-blink and close

vi.

Seeing is memory we ignore
When sung, when drowned, upended
Bridges water names

Painting is color petting a body
Mornings never unclasp

Diligent tongue arched
Spider, gossamer
Lilac hand-frond

Acknowledgements:

The author wishes to extend thanks to journals and editors who initially published excerpts from this book. Thank you *Blackbox Manifold*, *Conjunctions*, *Hurricane Review*, *The Oakland Review*, *Posit*, *SplitLevel Journal*, Alex Houen, Jamey Jones, Karla Kelsey, Susan Lewis, Aaron McCollough, Bradford Morrow, Adam Piette, and Lauren Shapiro. Special thanks to Lei Yanni, and to everyone at Omnidawn for attention and care taken with this book. My gratitude to Rusty Morrison for ongoing support of my work, and to Laura Joakimson, Sophia Carr, and Sharon Zetter.

LAYNIE BROWNE's recent books include: *Everyone & Her Resemblances* (Pamenar 2024), *Intaglio Daughters* (Ornithopter 2023), *Practice Has No Sequel* (Pamenar 2023), *Letters Inscribed in Snow* (Tinderbox 2023), and *Translation of the Lilies Back into Lists* (Wave Books, 2022). Her work has appeared in journals such as *Conjunctions, A Public Space, New American Writing, The Brooklyn Rail*, and in anthologies including: *The Ecopoetry Anthology* (Trinity University Press), *The Reality Street Book of Sonnets* (Reality Street, UK), and *Postmodern American Poetry: A Norton Anthology* (W.W. Norton). Her honors include a 2014 Pew Fellowship, the National Poetry Series Award (2007), for her collection *The Scented Fox*, and the Contemporary Poetry Series Award (2005) for her book *Drawing of a Swan Before Memory*. She edited the anthology *A Forest on Many Stems: Essays on the Poet's Novel* (Nightboat 2021) and co-edited the anthology *I'll Drown My Book: Conceptual Writing by Women* (Les Figues 2012). Recent collaborations include a public art project, "Dawn Chorus," a curated constellation of poetry in thirteen languages by twenty-eight writers engraved in The Rail Park in Philadelphia with visual artist Brent Wahl. In 2024 a solo show of her collage titled "On the Way to the Filmic Woods" was exhibited at the Brodsky Gallery at Kelly Writer's House. She teaches at University of Pennsylvania.

Apprentice to a Breathing Hand
by Laynie Browne

Cover design by Sharon Zetter
Cover typeface: Garamond 3 LT & Minion Pro
Interior design by Sharon Zetter
Interior typefaces: Balthazar & Garamond 3 LT

Printed in the United States
by Books International, Dulles, Virginia
Acid Free Archival Quality Recycled Paper

Publication of this book was made possible in part by gifts from
Katherine & John Gravendyk in honor of Hillary Gravendyk,
Francesca Bell, Mary Mackey, and The New Place Fund

Omnidawn Publishing Oakland, California
Staff and Volunteers, Spring 2025
Rusty Morrison & Laura Joakimson, co-publishers
Rob Hendricks, poetry & fiction editor,
& post-pub marketing
Jeffrey Kingman, copy editor
Sharon Zetter, poetry editor & book designer
Anthony Cody, poetry editor
Liza Flum, poetry editor
Rayna Carey, poetry editor
Sophia Carr, production editor
Elizabeth Aeschliman, fiction & poetry editor
Jennifer Metsker, marketing assistant
Avantika Chitturi, marketing assistant
Angela Liu, marketing assistant